To my dear fashionable Princess —

every teen girl's little pink book

on what to wear

not that you need any help

by Cathy Bartel

GW00669806

Harrison House
Tulsa, Oklahoma

12 11 10 09 08   15 14 13 12 11 10 9 8 7 6 5 4

every teen girl's little pink book on what to wear
ISBN 13: 978-1-57794-795-0
ISBN 10: 1-57794-795-9
Copyright © 2006 by Cathy Bartel
P.O. Box 691923
Tulsa, Oklahoma 74179

Published by Harrison House, Inc.
P.O. Box 35035
Tulsa, Oklahoma 74153

contents

go to the Father

Dear Friend,

Ever since I can remember, my Dad took an interest in my wardrobe. I have such fond memories of him taking me shopping for my back-to-school clothes. He didn't take me every year, but quite often he did—especially when I was younger.

I remember one time he picked out an outfit for me; and even though I didn't think it was that cool, I felt proud to wear it because he had taken an interest in shopping with me. Even as I got older, my dad was the greatest at picking out the nicest gifts, many of which were clothing items. I remember when I was about to get married, Dad gave me some money and told me to spruce up my wardrobe a bit. What a blessing!

My dad went to heaven several years ago and, oh, how I miss him! But I am thankful for the example he was in kindness and thoughtfulness, always giving. Everyone who knew him would say how kindhearted he was.

Now, you might be thinking, *That sure is nice for you! My dad has never done anything like that,* or, *I don't even have a dad.* There are different circumstances. Not all dads take their daughters shopping. Not all dads show their daughters affection, but that doesn't mean they don't love their daughters with all their heart. And then there are some of us who don't even have a dad. Either he has died, or we've never met him. Maybe you know him, but you don't have a relationship with him. I'm so sorry if you are in one of these situations.

Now please give me your ear for a moment. You may have heard this before, but I am going to tell you again because it bears repeating. This is a truth that will help you for the rest of your life. Whether you have a good dad, bad dad, or no dad, you have a heavenly Father who created you and is interested in every part of your life. He is always available to help you and meet your every need! Your part in this is to receive His love and trust Him with your life. Every part of it! Trust Him with your family, your relationships, your school, your future, and even what you wear. He cares about everything you care about. What a wonderful Father! Just think about all He has done for us. Let's bring honor to Him as we clothe ourselves both inside and out.

Love,
Cathy

think pink

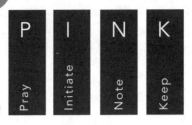

P — Pray
I — Initiate
N — Note
K — Keep

Lord, I thank You for making me and making me well. I am not an accident. You formed me in my mother's womb. You have given me a future. You designed me for great things. I am determined to do Your will and not miss out on the plans You have for me. I love You, Lord, and I am so thankful to be Your daughter.

Know, first, who you are; and then adorn yourself accordingly.

—Epictetus[i]

> Those who look to him for help will be radiant with joy; no shadow of shame will darken their faces.
>
> *Psalm 34:5 NLT*

As you look to the Lord and seek Him about everything that concerns you, He promises to help you. The Bible says, "I looked for the Lord, and He answered me. And He took away all my fears. They looked to Him and their faces shined with joy. Their faces will never be ashamed" (Ps. 34:4,5 NLV). That's the true way to shine!

When we're confident in our God as His daughters, we truly radiate His light and love to others. Knowing you are forgiven and you have let the Lord work in your heart, you will radiate joy, peace, and kindness that no brand of makeup or accessory can imitate. These beautiful qualities truly work from the inside out.

At the same time, remember that the Lord wants you to have fun, so enjoy all the pretty things He has blessed you with. It's always fun to get some new lip gloss, a new pair of earrings, or even a cute pair of socks. (I just love a cute pair of socks!) All these things help to make us feel pretty. Just remember not to overdo it and hide the real you. Let the personality God gave you shine.

we wear our hair

I'm not proud to say this, but I have a lot of hair stories I could tell you. I'm coming clean right now! Sometimes I've gotten overly concerned about hair. There have been *too* many times! I admit it: At times I have not been patient, should have prayed, and have just gotten foolishly carried away with a pair of scissors or a bottle of bleach—and sometimes several colors.

One time in particular, I went dark brown. It was much too dark for me. The next morning, I put on a hat and went to my friendly neighborhood beauty supply (a place that should ban people like me) and bought something to tone down the color. I toned it down all right—to an "I Love Lucy" red! Then I put my Red Baron hat back on, returned to the store, and loaded up on bleach!

By the time I was done that day, my hair had been burgundy, tomato red, orange, green, yellow, and finally white. Needless to say, my scalp was raw. Ouch! I had a good sense of humor for the first couple days. But on the third day, as I stood on the driveway, waving goodbye to my husband as he left for work, the tears started squirting out of my eyes. It just wasn't funny anymore. My head hurt. My pride hurt. I was so embarrassed. Really, what it came down to was that I was furious with myself!

My husband got out of the car, gave me a big hug, and told me, "Everything will be fine." I said, "Thank you," but thought, *Yeah, it'll be fine as long as I stay in this house for about three months....*

A couple hours later, the doorbell rang. As I sheepishly opened the door, a woman from the florist held out a dozen roses. These weren't just any roses. They were quite an assortment: pink, purple, yellow, blue, green, burgundy, red, orange, and even white! The little note attached said, "Honey, I love you no matter what color you are. With all my love forever, Blaine."

I guess I don't have to tell you that I started crying again. This time, though, they were tears of joy. I got my sense of humor back, thanks to the sweet blonde-haired, blue-eyed man I'm so thankful and proud to call my husband! God love him!

The next day, I was able to get an appointment with a gal who was very good with color. I was so thankful to get my old hair back. I then sent *her* a dozen roses!

I shouldn't have messed with my hair to begin with. Do you ever do foolish things like that? I'll pray for you, and please pray for me to not worry about my hair! I'm working on it.

God is so good. I have to say that when I received those flowers from Blaine, it was such a reminder to me that God looks on our hearts and loves us no matter how we look. What a good Father! He also helps us fix things that we've messed up!

Trust Him more than you ever have. He is interested in everything that concerns you! You're the apple of His eye! You are tattooed on the palm of His hand. Wow!

think pink

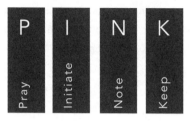

PINK

P — Pray
I — Initiate
N — Note
K — Keep

1 PETER 3:3, 4 NLT

Don't be concerned about the outward beauty that depends on fancy hairstyles, expensive jewelry, or beautiful clothes. You should be known for the beauty that comes from within, the unfading beauty of a gentle and quiet spirit, which is so precious to God.

People seldom notice old clothes if you wear a big smile.

—Lee Mildon[ii]

5 marks of a confident person

Use this as a check to see if you are confident in who you are in Christ.

 You aren't afraid to meet new people.

 You like to try new things and see new places.

 You aren't afraid to take calculated risks in order to achieve something you want.

 You don't get discouraged and depressed when you fail. Instead, you pick yourself back up.

 It doesn't bother you much when people criticize you.

If all 5 of the statements above describe you, then you are very confident. If 4 of the statements are true about you, then your confidence is solid and improving. If 3 of the statements are true, then your confidence could use some improvement. It's not looking good if only 2 statements are true; you are limiting yourself from great experiences. If you only found 1 statement to be true, reread this book until all the statements are true. Remember: In Christ, you are a new creation.

> ...those who become Christians become new persons. They are not the same anymore, for the old life is gone. A new life has begun!
>
> 2 Corinthians 5:17 NLT

dress sharp,
smell pretty,
& change
someone's life!

I'd like you to take a moment and think about the woman why you think dresses sharp and smells pretty. Let me explain. I have always had a woman in my life whom I've admired. Sometimes we look at a person and think, *Oh, my! She dresses so nice,* and the more we get to know her, it's not so much her appearance but her character and heart that we admire.

For example, when I was growing up, there was a lady in my neighborhood named Rosie. She and her husband, Larry, had four kids I went to school with. I always loved getting to spend time with Rosie because she genuinely loved young people. She would arrange to get our junior high gym opened on Friday nights so we'd have something to do. She also opened up her home many, many Friday nights just so we'd have a safe place to hang out, play ping pong, listen to music, and talk.

One thing about Rosie that I'll never forget is that she always smelled so pretty. I'm ashamed to admit that one time when I was over there, I snooped around in the bathroom to see if I could find what kind of perfume she wore. I just wanted to smell like Rosie. When I got older I finally just asked one time and she told me, and I've been wearing that brand ever since.

Looking back, I realize that as lovely as the perfume was, it was her life that was the sweet fragrance. She was a Christian, and her heart was dressed with the real, genuine love of Christ. She clothed herself with compassion, kindness, humility, and a quiet strength. She wore the love of God, and anyone who was around her breathed in an exquisite fragrance! *The Message Bible* calls it "a sweet scent rising to God" (2 Cor. 2:15). That's what I recognized.

When I was about 14 years old, I prayed, "Lord, I want to be like Rosie," not knowing that I would marry a man who would minister to teens all over the world or that many times my own living room and home would be filled with young people. One night, we had a group of kids in our home and Blaine had a pile of devotionals in our front entryway ready to hand out to every young person as they left. As I looked over at the devotionals from the back of my living room, my eyes filled with tears of joy. I took a little moment by myself and said, "Thank You, Lord, for letting me be like Rosie." You see, whenever Rosie had young people in her home, she made sure they left with a Bible and devotional.

God places wonderful people in our lives to admire and form desires in our hearts of things we can do to be a blessing. For the past 25 years, I have admired another woman. She is my pastor's wife. She always looks great and dresses sharp. She just knows how to pull an outfit together—all the accessories, the right shoes and purse, and so forth. But do you know what I admire most in her? She is a very wise woman and is an example of stability to me. That's what I have learned most from her.

She is a woman who has built her home and family on the Word of God. Proverbs 24:3 AMP says, "Through skillful and godly Wisdom is a house (a life, a home, a family) built, and by understanding it is established [on a sound and good foundation], and by knowledge shall its chambers...be filled with all precious and pleasant riches."

Because she has taken time to dress sharp on the inside, her life has been a blessing to her husband and all of her children, who serve God. She is a wonderful grandmother and godly example to thousands of women.

My point is that you, as God's daughter, are never too young to dress sharp and smell pretty and make your life count. First Timothy 4:12 NIV says, "Don't let anyone look down on you because you are young, but set an example for the believers in speech, in life, in love, in faith and in purity." Someone is looking to you to help her live her life. You can lead her to Jesus by how you present yourself to this world.

There is nothing more beautiful than a young woman who is happy and loves God with all of her heart, soul, mind, and strength. We have been given a responsibility to represent Him in a manner that brings honor to Him. Let's be reminded of what Jesus has done for us. He has bestowed on us a crown of beauty instead of ashes, the oil of gladness instead of mourning, and a garment of praise instead of a spirit of despair.

How about it? Let's clothe ourselves in Christ and for Christ—and change someone's life.

think pink

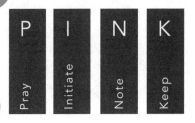

P — Pray
I — Initiate
N — Note
K — Keep

This little light of mine, I'm gonna let it shine. Shine those lips, glow those cheeks, glitter those eyes, flash that jewelry! All these things are so fun to do (if Mom and Dad say it's okay). Just remember: Less is more, and you are beautiful from the inside out.

It's the joy of the Lord that people are really going to notice. If you have real joy on your life, the joy that comes from knowing the Lord, then you will be able to share that with a beautiful smile. His joy gives you strength and confidence. When you wear His joy, you wear one of the most important accessories ever—a beautiful, contagious smile. Let me tell you: That is a piece of jewelry that reaches deep down in others' hearts and truly makes you stand out from the rest!

While clothes may not make the woman, they certainly have a strong effect on her self-confidence—which, I believe, does make the woman.

—Mary Kay Ash[iii]

Think about some of these words. They don't define who you are, but they may describe your style—and some of them are just fun to say! What's your style?

Elegant	With-it
Graceful	Preppy
Sporty	Classy
Polished	Sharp
Sophisticated	Up-to-date
Chic	Cute
Casual	Cool
Urban	Formal
Hip	Informal
Happening	Trendy

dare wear

Did you know that the Bible tells you how to dress? It's not about the outward appearance, but about the inward appearance. When we dress our inner person, our outward appearance lines up. Ephesians 6 shows us how to dress our inner person by putting on the armor of God.

> Use every piece of God's armor to resist the enemy in the time of evil, so that after the battle you will still be standing firm. Stand your ground, putting on the sturdy belt of truth....
>
> *Ephesians 6:13,14 NLT*

I call the first piece of armor *dare wear.* It's the belt of truth. You've maybe played "Truth or Dare." Well, in this case the choice is to dare to tell the truth and to live your life by truth. When we dress our inner person in truth, we never have to hide anything from anyone. It is freedom. When you are faced with a decision of whether to tell the truth or not, remember that truth is freedom. Be honest, and be who you are. Don't live a lie, trying to be what someone wants you to be. Dare to be real, and put on the belt of truth every day.

think pink

P — Pray

I — Initiate

N — Note

K — Keep

PROVERBS
31:30 MSG

Charm can mislead and beauty
soon fades. The woman to be admired
and praised is the woman who lives
in the Fear-of-God.

People are ridiculous only when they try or seem to be that which they are not.

—Giacomo Leopard[iiv]

3 ways to discover who you are

Perhaps one of the greatest journeys that you'll ever take is the one that leads you to the discovery of who God created you to be. You have a unique personality and skill set that God has given you. Many young people fail to realize all that God has made them to be. Here are 3 things to remember in this exciting journey.

 You will be incomplete without Christ.

Just as God puts 2 people together in marriage, He wants you to be married to Christ. Without that ongoing relationship with Jesus, you will always come up short.

 Study carefully what God has said about you.

The Bible is full of Scriptures that describe the attributes and character that He has for you as a person. The Word of God is like a mirror. (James 1:23.) When you look at it and commit to do it, you take on the character of God.

3. *Talk to family and friends about your unique personality.*

Many times other people see things in us that we fail to recognize. You may be a great organizer, counselor, leader, giver, creator, or helper. Most of the time people around you will recognize that gift more quickly than you will.

the looking glass

Hebrews 1:3 says that Jesus "perfectly mirrors God, and is stamped with God's nature. He holds everything together by what He says—powerful words" (MSG). As we read God's Word and dress ourselves in it, we are literally being changed from the inside out and are stamped with God's nature. God's Word is a mirror of how He wants us to be. The more it becomes a part of us, the more we reflect His message of life and love to others.

Sometimes we look in the Word and see something we need to change in our hearts. We may discover a bad attitude, jealousy, depression, envy, hatred, or just plain old sin in our lives. At the same time, when we look in the Word, we see our greatest potential—all that God has done for us and what He wants to do through us. God works His Word in us to will and to do His good pleasure.

God's Word is a faith mirror. It shows us what we can be when we reach for our God-given potential by faith. For instance, don't you want to reflect His love? Well, see yourself as a girl who does what 1 Corinthians 13 says.

> Love suffers long *and* is kind; love does not envy; love does not parade itself, is not puffed up; does not behave rudely, does not seek its own, is not provoked, thinks no evil; does not rejoice in iniquity, but rejoices in the truth; bears all things, believes all things, hopes all things, endures all things. Love never fails.
>
> 1 Corinthians 13:4-8 NKJV

Now memorize this Scripture. See yourself as God sees you—as His daughter who loves.

We want to honor our Father by reflecting the truth we have been taught in His Word. Let's do it. James tells us not to look in the mirror and forget what we've seen. We need to be responsible to put to practice what we've been taught and what we've read.

Proverbs 27:19 NLT says, "As a face is reflected in water, so the heart reflects the person!" Let's shine God's love on people. Let's spend more time in our heart mirror (the Word of God) than in our bathroom mirror. As I'm writing this to you, I'm checking on myself, too.

Now, what do we do about those bathroom mirrors and full-length mirrors? They're everywhere, and we have to like what we see there, too.

A few years ago, we moved into a beautiful new home. I have enjoyed it so much, but when we first got here I had to get used to our new bathroom. Talk about mirrors! They were everywhere. In fact, there was a whole wall of mirrors. I didn't like getting out of the tub or shower at first. Let me tell you, I would grab a towel or robe as quickly as you could say "treadmill"!

It can sometimes be humbling to look at what we came into the world in (our birthday suits)! Just grasp a hold of the fact now, while you are young, that your body has been changing from the day you were born and will continue to change. We are to be so thankful for our bodies! It's so important that when you look in the mirror, you absolutely know how much God loves you throughout every season of your life.

Maybe you're reading this book and your body is going through all kinds of changes. You're growing up. I don't have any daughters, but I was one (well, I still am one) and I am so thankful I had a precious mom who celebrated my teen years with me. I hope you have a wonderful mom, or someone close to you, who can help you through the changes you're experiencing.

God knows you and your body better than anyone else does. Start trusting Him now because as a woman you go through many seasons and He will help you to remain strong and steady throughout each one. He will see us through all of our changes. Thank You, Lord!

If you have any questions about how precious you are to God, read the Scripture below.

> O Lord, you have examined my heart and know everything about me. You know when I sit down or stand up. You know my every thought when far away. You chart the path ahead of me and tell me where to stop and rest. Every moment you know where I am. You know what I am going to say even before I say

it, Lord. You both precede and follow me. You place your hand of blessing on my head. Such knowledge is too wonderful for me, too great for me to know! I can never escape from your spirit! I can never get away from your presence! If I go up to heaven, you are there; if I go down to the place of the dead, you are there. If I ride the wings of the morning, if I dwell by the farthest oceans, even there your hand will guide me, and your strength will support me. I could ask the darkness to hide me and the light around me to become night—but even in darkness I cannot hide from you. To you the night shines as bright as day. Darkness and light are both alike to you. You made all the delicate, inner parts of my body and knit me together in my mother's womb. Thank you for making me so wonderfully complex! Your workmanship is marvelous—and how well I know it. You watched me as I was being formed in utter seclusion, as I was woven together in the dark of the womb. You saw me before I was born. Every day of my life was recorded in your book. Every moment was laid out before a single day had passed. How precious are your thoughts about me, O God! They are innumerable! I can't even count them; they outnumber the grains of sand! And when I wake up in the morning, you are still with me!

Psalm 139:1-18 NLT

We have to be thankful and comfortable in our own skin before we can really be comfortable in our clothes! We are spirits, we have souls, and we live in these precious bodies God created. If you're unhappy with how you look, start right now by saying, "Lord, I surrender my heart and my body to You. Thank You for making me and believing in me. I know You love me."

think pink

P - Pray
I - Initiate
N - Note
K - Keep

1 CORINTHIANS
6:19,20 NIV

Do you not know that your body is the temple of the Holy Spirit, who is in you, whom you have received from God? You are not your own; you were bought at a price. Therefore honor God with your body.

Wear a smile and have friends; wear a scowl and have wrinkles.

—George Eliot[v]

mirror

For if any be a hearer of the word, and not a doer, he is like unto a man beholding his natural face in a glass: for he beholdeth himself, and goeth his way, and straightway forgetteth what manner of man he was.

James 1:23,24

Many of today's young people have a distorted view of who they really are. Some have believed the lie that humans are little more than monkeys that are "fully loaded" with all the options.

Do you remember going to the fair and walking through the maze of mirrors? Some would make you look tiny, while others made you look as tall as Venus and Serena Williams. Others just made you look plain weird and twisted.

To get a proper perspective on who we really are, we've got to look into a mirror that will give us an accurate and truthful reflection. That mirror is the Word of God. However, when we walk away from God's mirror, we have to remember what kind of person His Word wants us to be. That means that when we look into God's Word, we've got to take more than a casual glance; we need to look with diligent focus.

bear wear

The second piece of God's armor for our inner person is the breastplate of righteousness. (Eph. 6:14.) And yes, a breastplate covers your breasts. I call this *bear wear*. God desires to protect your body, because when you *bear* more than you should it's really you that is hurt in the end. Your body is important to God, and He has intended it for the man you marry.

The breastplate also covers your heart. It protects your feelings and emotions. God calls it the breastplate of righteousness. Righteousness means that when you have accepted Jesus as your Lord, His righteousness becomes your righteousness. You are in right standing with God. You can come to Him at any time and bare your soul to Him. If you are hurting and broken, then you can come to Him and receive healing—emotionally and physically. You have the right to cry out to God, and He as your loving Father will answer you, *bear* your concerns, and heal your broken heart.

This powerful piece of armor also allows you to *bear* up under the attacks of the enemy. There are people who can be enemies, and then there is the enemy of your soul who is busy trying to twist people's words and situations to make you feel unworthy and useless. But God has given you His breastplate of righteousness, so you know you are important to Him and useful to His kingdom. Your value is in who you are in Christ, not what someone else thinks of you. So remind yourself whom you belong to, and put on the breastplate of righteousness every day.

think pink

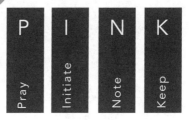

P Pray
I Initiate
N Note
K Keep

PSALM 37:3-5 NKJV

Trust in the Lord, and do good;
dwell in the land, and feed on
His faithfulness. Delight
yourself also in the Lord, and
He shall give you the desires of
your heart. Commit your way to
the Lord, trust also in Him,
and He shall bring it to pass.

To have that sense of one's intrinsic worth which constitutes self-respect is potentially to have everything.

—Joan Didion[vi]

the popularity trap

And do not be conformed to this world, but be transformed by the renewing of your mind, that you may prove what is that good and acceptable and perfect will of God.

Romans 12:2 NKJV

The world promotes popularity, and it's easy to get caught up in wearing the right clothes and driving the right car to be accepted. It's all just a trap that makes you feel insecure in yourself. But when you discover who you are in Christ, your inner person is strengthened. The pressures of the world cannot crush you into their mold. You begin to experience the freedom that can only be found in Christ Jesus. If you have been struggling with your self-worth, then take some time to find out who you are in Christ. Look up all the Scriptures in the New Testament epistles that say "in Him," "in whom," or "in Christ."

Pray this prayer:

Lord, I do not want to be conformed to this world, but I want to be transformed by the renewing of my mind. Help me to understand who I am in Christ Jesus. Help me to break away from the negative influences of the world that damage my self-worth. Ground me in Your love and faithfulness, in Jesus' name.

what guys really want

I recently read a letter by a Christian 17-year-old young man who wrote in to a girls' magazine. Basically he was letting Christian girls know that the way they dress really does affect young men. He said that he and his brothers in Christ want to respect girls and to be pure with their thoughts, eyes, and actions. He wanted young women to consider how the way they dress influences guys.

I really admire this young man for writing this, and I encourage you to wear things that are not too short, not too tight, and not too low. That is part of walking in the love of God.

When we dress to please God, we not only bring respect to ourselves but we can also be a wonderful influence and example to others.

think pink

P Pray
I Initiate
N Note
K Keep

Lord, You laid down Your life for me. Surely I can choose to dress to please You. When I dress to please You, I believe I am walking in the love of God. I'll be an example to other young women. I will represent You to the people I am around. When I am around young men, they can look at me and see a godly young woman. In Jesus' name I pray. Amen.

Clothes make the man.
Naked people have
little or no influence
on society.

—Mark Twain[vii]

wear wisely

Your parents, your youth leaders, your pastors, and I just want to remind you how important it is to be wise in what you wear. It's not to be bossy or annoying. More than anything, it is to protect you. No one wants to take the fun and fab out of your wardrobe. Your style is a great way to express your personality and have your own distinctive appearance. Just be sure you wear clothes that would be pleasing to your Father God.

pair wear

The third piece of God's armor is a pair of shoes! I call this *pair wear*. Girls love shoes, and I thank God we have lots to choose from! He made us this way, you know. We are supposed to look good. It's really fun, and I'm glad that is part of our design.

God gave us some amazing shoes for our inner person. He tells us in the Scriptures that they are the shoes of peace.

> For shoes, put on the peace that comes from the Good News, so that you will be fully prepared.
>
> Ephesians 6:15 NLT

The shoes for our inner person come from the Good News of Jesus Christ. That news is that He came to save us from sin, from sickness, and from death. He came to give us life—abundant life here on the earth and eternal life in heaven. When we put these shoes on, we put on the peace that our eternal destiny is secure.

When we on put these shoes, we also put on love for others. As you remind yourself every day of your spiritual shoes, you prepare yourself to share the Good News of Jesus with each person God leads you to. That may not always mean leading someone to Christ, but it may mean being nice to someone you don't know or encouraging someone who is down. Listen inside to what God is directing you to do. Look for ways to reach out to others. The book of Romans tells us that those who share the Good News of Jesus have beautiful feet.

> And how can they preach unless they are sent? As it is written, "How beautiful are the feet of those who bring good news!"
>
> *Romans 10:15 NIV*

We have some fine shoes to wear! God is absolutely interested in what we wear inside and out, so give His love to others with that certain flair He has put in you!

think pink

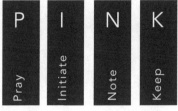

P — Pray
I — Initiate
N — Note
K — Keep

PSALM 16:11 MSG

Now you've got my feet on
the life path, all radiant from
the shining of your face.
Ever since you took my hand,
I'm on the right way.

There may be those on earth who dress better or eat better, but those who enjoy the peace of God sleep better.

L. Thomas Holdcroft[viii]

3 ways to put on Christ and make friends

Everyone wants to be liked. People want friends, and everyone—even the one who seems a little "stuck up"—wants to be friendly. When you put on Christ by genuinely caring about others, you'll make friends.

 Be friendly.

It seems obvious, but many people get so focused on the task in front of them that they miss the people and possible relationships passing them by. Grab each opportunity to build new relationships by doing the small things that make it happen. Say hello, introduce yourself, or simply smile. Make the first effort by showing yourself friendly. (Prov. 18:24.)

 Focus on others.

People want to talk about things that matter to them. If you spend 4 hours talking about your last doctor's appointment to someone you just met, don't be surprised if they start avoiding you. Make the effort to find out what they like, and focus on things that you have in common.

3. *Do kind things without looking for credit.*

The simple principle of sowing and reaping works in friendships too. If you begin to go out of your way to sow into people's lives, you will begin to reap the kind of friends you want. (Gal. 6:7.)

not sew
perfect

When I was about 12 years old, I decided I would like to take up sewing. I had taken a few little home economics classes at school, my Grandma Hunt had given me her old pedal sewing machine, and I was so excited to get started.

First I made a dress that looked somewhat like a flour sack. You may ask, "Did you want to wear it?" Yes, I did. I was very proud of my accomplishment. I didn't care what I looked like!

My next attempt was a blue and white gingham blouse. One day when I was working on it after school, the whole process became so frustrating that at one point I cussed! And I cussed some more! My little brother heard me and told on me, and I was grounded for two weeks! To top it off, the first day I wore that blouse to school my math teacher walked by, noticed a thread hanging on my shoulder, and gave it a little tug. My sleeve proceeded to unravel, and the whole thing fell off!

I guess that's when I decided to stick to shopping. I enjoyed it a lot more and didn't get grounded for cussing.

My sweet little grandma went to heaven several years ago, but I still have her sewing machine. It's in my living room. That old machine is a constant reminder of how thankful I am to the Lord for helping me to clean up my mouth. It's also the reminder of my little gray-haired, rosy-cheeked Grandma who never said a bad word about anyone, let alone a cuss word!

I've never tried sewing again, and I absolutely know it's not my gift. But I sure do admire people who do. Whether you like to make your own clothes or purchase them, or a little of both, have some fun doing it. Just remember how much God loves you, and honor Him with your words and your wardrobe.

think pink

P **Pray**
I **Initiate**
N **Note**
K **Keep**

ROMANS 12:1 NLT

And so, dear brothers and sisters,
I plead with you to give your bodies
to God. Let them be a living and
holy sacrifice—the kind he will accept.
When you think of what he has done
for you, is it too much to ask?

No one can make you
feel inferior without
your consent.

—Eleanor Roosevelt[ix]

3 musts for building real confidence

If you need more confidence in your life, here is a simple game plan that will help you grow.

1. Find your identity in Christ Jesus.

If we look to ourselves for confidence, we have many reasons to be insecure and disappointed. But in Christ, we are amazing. Look up these Scriptures: 2 Corinthians 5:17; Philippians 4:13; Colossians 1:22; Jude 24; Romans 8:15.

2. Surround yourself with people who believe in you.

Small people criticize big dreams. Don't allow your faith and self-esteem to be robbed by critical or negative people. Surround yourself with people who believe in you.

3. Take small steps to build big victories.

We all have things in our lives we are secretly afraid of. Maybe it's heights, meeting new people, trying new foods, or sharing your faith. Don't take a leap of faith; take little steps toward overcoming your fears. The Bible says, "The steps of a good man are ordered by the Lord" (Ps. 37:23 NKJV).

Build these 3 steps to confidence into your daily routine, and watch your confidence soar.

glare wear

The fourth piece of God's armor is the shield of faith. As you live by your belief in Jesus as your Savior, faith rises in your inner person. I call this *glare wear.* It's like God's bling! When your faith is strong, it glares like a shiny shield, protecting you from the attacks of the enemy.

> In every battle you will need faith as your shield to stop the fiery arrows aimed at you by Satan.

> *Ephesians 6:16 NLT*

This shield of faith is seen through your attitude. Faith will not let you sink into self-pity when things don't go your way. Faith stands strong, knowing that God has the best in mind for you and is helping you to achieve it.

Especially when people come against you with their words, it can feel just like sharp arrows piercing into you. People say that sticks and stones can break bones but words will never hurt you, but the truth is that words can truly hurt you. If you don't have your shield of faith up and ready, words can damage your self-worth and drop you into depression. God's will is for you to live in victory. He gave you *glare wear,* so you can fight off those arrows with faith in God!

think pink

P I N K

Pray Initiate Note Keep

Z E P H A N I A H   3 : 1 7   N L T

For the Lord your God has arrived to live among you. He is a mighty savior. He will rejoice over you with great gladness. With his love, he will calm all your fears. He will exult over you by singing a happy song.

It ain't what they
call you, it's what
you answer to.

—W.C. Fields[x]

7 personal beliefs that will alter your future

Without a doubt, the most important thing you can establish in your life right now is what you believe—your faith in God. Your core convictions will separate you from the pack.

I believe I am God's child and He is my Father. (1 John 3:1.)

I believe the Holy Spirit leads me in all my decisions. (Rom. 8:14.)

I believe I am more than a conqueror in every challenge life brings. (Rom. 8:37.)

I believe God is the author of my promotion in every area of life. (Ps. 75:6,7.)

I believe that when I pray, God hears me and answers me. (Mark 11:24.)

I believe that as I meditate on God's Word, He makes my way prosperous. (Josh. 1:8.)

I believe that nothing is impossible because I believe. (Mark 9:23.)

let's talk shop!

Did you realize that your heavenly Father is very interested in your shopping adventures? I say adventures because they certainly can be.

He wants you to find great bargains, and remember this:

When you delight yourself in the Lord, He will give you the desires of your heart. Don't ever hesitate to ask the Lord to help you find the dress for that special event or that great pair of jeans! He will give you wisdom and lead you so you don't have to waste a lot of time looking.

You are His daughter, and you can hear His voice. Sometimes He will even prompt you to wait because there is a great sale you'll miss if you shop too soon. Other times He will speak to your heart to give something to someone, perhaps your sister or girlfriend or little cousin who looks up to you.

It can be the most fun ever just to bless someone out of the blue. It can bring you so much joy to give someone a gift—not a birthday or Christmas gift, but just a gift to remind her that you are thinking of her and to let her know that God put her on your heart. It could be a T-shirt, a cute pair of socks, maybe a little purse, something for her hair, or even a gift card. Be sensitive to the Lord, and He will tell you what to do. The Lord can help us be thoughtful. He loves it when we give to others and think about others. That's totally being His daughter. He is so proud of us when we act like Him. He says, "That's My girl!"

Okay, how about asking Him to give us wisdom in the dressing room? Remember: I love you. Take a good look at those hem lines and let the Lord be your guideline so you don't end up in the headlines!

Listen to your heart. God will help you make good choices in the dressing rooms and in the stores. When you take His help, now that's smart shopping!

think pink

P Pray
I Initiate
N Note
K Keep

COLOSSIANS
3:12 MSG

So, chosen by God for this new
life of love, dress in the wardrobe
God picked out for you:
compassion, kindness, humility,
quiet strength, discipline.

Keeping your clothes
well pressed will keep
you from looking
hard pressed.

—Coleman Co[xxi]

put on

But above all these things put on love, which is the bond of perfection.

Colossians 3:14 NKJV

There are things that we "put on" every day. We put on our clothes, put on a coat, put on makeup, put on a retainer.... You get it. The truth is that there are times we don't always feel like "putting on" some of these things.

Love is the same way. We don't always feel like showing it. Love isn't a feeling. It's a choice we make for the good of others. That's exactly why God tells us to put it on whether we feel like it or not. So every morning, wake up, get out of bed, and put on love.

fair wear

The fifth piece of God's armor is the helmet of salvation. (Eph. 6:17.) When Jesus died to bring us salvation, He was working to restore us and make us whole. Salvation means that nothing is missing and nothing is broken. It includes provision, health, and wholeness of mind, body, and spirit.

In the armor of God, salvation is represented as a helmet—a covering over your face and your mind. I call this *fair wear*—fair because as girls we like to take care of our faces. We like to use cleansers, moisturizers, makeup, and all kinds of things to make our faces look better. It's the first thing people see, and we want it to look its best.

The definition of "fair" is "pleasing to the eye or mind especially because of fresh, charming, or flawless quality."[xii] Not only do we want our faces to be pleasing, but we also want our minds to be pleasing. God gave us a helmet of salvation to protect our minds.

Our thoughts can be so damaging if we let them roam in the wrong direction. When we understand that salvation has so many good things for us, we can train our thoughts to come back on course and stay positive. The book of Philippians helps us to know what thoughts will help us to live successful and happy lives.

> Finally, brethren, whatever things are true, whatever things are noble, whatever things are just, whatever things are pure, whatever things are lovely, whatever things are of good report, if there is any virtue and if there is anything praiseworthy—meditate on these things.
>
> *Philippians 4:8 NKJV*

When you put on your *fair wear,* you determine to keep your thoughts going in a positive direction and you set the course for a great life!

think pink

P Pray
I Initiate
N Note
K Keep

1 CORINTHIANS
2:16 AMP

But we have the mind of Christ
(the Messiah) and do hold the
thoughts (feelings and purposes)
of His heart.

What a man thinks of himself, that is which determines, or rather indicates, his fate.

—Henry David Thoreau[xiii]

get this

Don't buy something just because of the label. Does the label make the clothes? You don't have to be a label name-dropper. If it's something you feel pretty in and it's in your budget, buy it—big name or not. Build a base of core elements in your wardrobe. Budget your money. Think before you buy, and remember that when you seek first the kingdom of God, all these things will be added unto you.

clean your closets

I challenge you to go through your wardrobe today and get rid of anything that belittles you. You know what I am talking about. Raise the standard. Set an example of how God's daughter should dress.

This will put it in perspective: Think ahead a few years from now, and ask yourself, "Am I dressing in a way that I would want my daughter to dress? Am I the kind of daughter that I want my daughter to be?" That's a little thought to consider for a while.

I am not a fashion consultant, but I fear the Lord and hate evil (Prov. 8:13), and I want to speak what is true into your life. I hate that the devil wants girls to think of themselves as unworthy.

When you get ready for the day, put on wisdom first. A great way to put on wisdom is to read the Proverbs. There are 31 Proverbs—one for each day of the month. Put on one of those in the morning just as you would a pair of jeans, your makeup, or your watch.

When you put God's Word on, you prepare yourself for life. You could think about it this way. When you need some lip gloss, you can pull it out of your purse if you've prepared and put it there. In the same way, when you need wisdom, you'll be able to find it in your heart because you prepared and put God's Word there.

When you look through your clothes to prepare for the day, remember to be realistic. Know your body type and your colors. Don't wear what you wish you looked good in; wear what really compliments you and what reflects who you are inside.

First Timothy 2:9 says that we are to wear decent and appropriate clothing, and the best way to make ourselves attractive is by doing good things. Instead of spending a lot of time primping before the mirror or chasing the latest fashion, we become beautiful by doing something beautiful for God and others.

I want to encourage you to let your inner beauty come out today. I love you and am so proud to be your sister in Christ. I know you want to please God in every area of your life. With a heart like that, you will!

think pink

P Pray
I Initiate
N Note
K Keep

Father, in the name of Jesus, I ask You to give me wisdom. Help me to dress my heart in Your Word. Help me to be diligent to study, and thank You for bringing back to my memory everything good that You put in my heart. As I spend time with You, I pray that people will know that I have been with You because my life is a sweet-smelling fragrance.

Put on the Word of God, just as you would a pair of jeans, every day!

It is remarkable how great an influence our clothes have on our moral state.

—Anatole France[xiv]

6 things you must believe about yourself

You will eventually become a product of what you believe. All great athletes, presidents, pastors, and corporate CEOs arrived where they are because they believed they could before anyone else believed in them. Here are 6 things you must believe about yourself.

 I have been given power over the devil. (1 John 4:4.)

 I have been given power over every circumstance in my life. (Mark 11:23.)

 I have a strong body that has been healed by the stripes taken on Jesus' back. (Matt. 8:17.)

 I have the ability to control my mind and cast out evil thoughts. (2 Cor. 10:4,5.)

 I am poised for success and will not accept any defeat as final. (1 Cor. 15:57.)

 I hate sin but love all people and have favor everywhere I go. (Prov. 12:2.)

care wear

The last piece of God's armor is the sword of the Spirit. (Eph. 6:17.) This sword represents the words that we speak and, specifically, the prayers that we pray. I call this *care wear*. It shows how much we care for others when we pray for them, and how much we care about serving God when we pray for our own lives. This part of our armor not only protects us from attacks, but it allows us to attack, too. What are we attacking? We are coming against the lies of the enemy and of the world that try to defeat us. The way we do this is to speak what God says, or to pray.

How can we know if we are praying the right thing? One way to make sure is to keep your prayers in line with what the Bible says. If you pray the same thing the Scripture says, you can be sure you are praying God's will. If the Scripture says that "no weapon formed against you shall prosper" (Isa. 54:17 NKJV), then you can pray this when someone comes against you. You might say, "Father God, thank You that the lies spoken against me will not prosper because You promised me this in Your Word."

Can you see how important it is to find out what God's Word says? Once you know the promise, you can pray it out in faith and then God can move to change the situation. Put on your *care wear* by reading and praying God's Word.

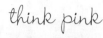

think pink

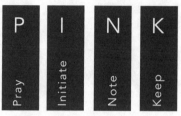

PROVERBS
31 : 26   N K J V

*She opens her mouth with
wisdom, and on her tongue
is the law of kindness.*

Speak clearly, if you
speak at all; carve
every word before
you let it fall.

—Oliver Wendell Holmes[xv]

6 practical actions of love toward others

God is love, and as imitators of Christ we are to put on love. Maybe you need some advice to get started. Here are some actions to get the ball rolling.

 1. *Be polite.*

Treat others with respect. Say "please" and "thank you."

 2. *Smile.*

Show off those pearly whites. This small gesture will go a long way.

 3. *Share.*

This unselfish act is packed with power.

 4. *Listen.*

Give others your full attention. They will appreciate the investment.

5. Lend a hand.

Mow the lawn for an elderly neighbor, or send a card to a relative you have been praying for.

6. Give a gift.

There doesn't have to be a special reason, but the best reason of all is to simply say, "I love you."

endnotes

[i]   http://www.quotegarden.com/clothing.html

[ii]   http://www.quotegarden.com/smiles.html

[iii]   www.zaadz.com/quotes/authors/mary_kay_ash/

[iv]   http://www.littlebluelight.com/lblphp/quotes.php?ikey=16

[v]   http://www.quotegarden.com/smiles.html

[vi]   *O, The Oprah Magazine,* May 2004.

[vii]   http://www.quotegarden.com/clothing.html

[viii]   http://www.brainyquote.com/quotes/quotes/l/lthomasho121903.html

[ix]   http://www.quotationspage.com/quote/137.html

[x]   http://www.quotegarden.com/confidence.html

[xi]   http://www.quotationspage.com/quotes/Coleman_Cox/

[xii]   http://www.m-w.com/dictionary/fair

[xiii]   http://www.quotegarden.com/confidence.html

[xiv]   http://www.zaadz.com/quotes/Anatole_France

[xv]   http://www.brainyquote.com/quotes/quotes/o/oliverwend122641.html

prayer of salvation

God loves you—no matter who you are, no matter what your past. God loves you so much that He gave His one and only begotten Son for you. The Bible tells us that "...whoever believes in him shall not perish but have eternal life" (John 3:16 NIV). Jesus laid down His life and rose again so that we could spend eternity with Him in heaven and experience His absolute best on earth. If you would like to receive Jesus into your life, say the following prayer out loud and mean it from your heart.

Heavenly Father, I come to You admitting that I am a sinner. Right now, I choose to turn away from sin, and I ask You to cleanse me of all unrighteousness. I believe that Your Son, Jesus, died on the cross to take away my sins. I also believe that He rose again from the dead so that I might be forgiven of my sins and made righteous through faith in Him. I call upon the name of Jesus Christ to be the Savior and Lord of my life. Jesus, I choose to follow You and ask that You fill me with the power of the Holy Spirit. I declare that right now I am a child of God. I am free from sin and full of the righteousness of God. I am saved in Jesus' name. Amen.

If you prayed this prayer to receive Jesus Christ as your Savior for the first time, please contact us on the Web at **www.harrisonhouse.com** to receive a free book.

Or you may write to us at

Harrison House
P.O. Box 35035 • Tulsa, Oklahoma 74153

about the author

For more than a quarter of a century, Cathy Bartel has served alongside her husband, Blaine, in what they believe is the hope of the world, the local church. For the better part of two decades, they have served their pastor, Willie George, in building one of America's most respected churches, Church on the Move, in Tulsa, Oklahoma. Most recently, they helped found Oneighty, which has become one of the most emulated youth ministries in the past 10 years, reaching 2,500–3,000 students weekly under their leadership.

While Blaine is known for his communication and leadership skills, Cathy is known for her heart and hospitality. Blaine is quick to recognize her "behind the scenes" gifting to lift and encourage people as one of the great strengths of their ministry together. Her effervescent spirit and contagious smile open the door for her ministry each day, whether she's in the church or at the grocery store.

Cathy is currently helping Blaine raise a new community of believers committed to relevant ministry and evangelism. Northstar Church will open its doors in the growing north Dallas suburb of Frisco, Texas, in the fall of 2006.

Cathy's greatest reward has come in the raising of her 3 boys—Jeremy, 21, Dillon, 19, and Brock, 17. Today, each son is serving Christ with his unique abilities and is deeply involved in Blaine and Cathy's ongoing ministry.

To contact Cathy Bartel please write to:

Cathy Bartel • Serving America's Future
P.O. Box 691923 • Tulsa, Oklahoma 74169
www.blainebartel.com

*Please include your prayer requests
and comments when you write.*

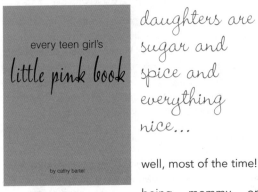

every teen girl's
little pink book

by cathy bartel

daughters are sugar and spice and everything nice...

well, most of the time!

being mommy or daddy's little *princess* can get challenging sometimes. plug into God's Word and discover what it means to be your heavenly Father's daughter and how special you are to your "fam."

stories, humor, scriptures...everything you need to become the lovely and hip *lady* God has destined you to be.

Available at fine bookstores everywhere or at **www.harrisonhouse.com**.

Harrison House
ISBN: 1-57794-792-4

every teen girl's
little pink book
on gab

by cathy bartel

g*irls*
a*bout to*
b*ecome*

what you think about,
you **gab** about, you
bring about. you will
become what you say.

launch your destiny simply by the things you say.
discover how to lay a foundation of success for
your future through your words – in love, in
school, in relationships, in life. become something great!

Available at fine bookstores everywhere or at
www.harrisonhouse.com.

Harrison House
ISBN: 1-57794-793-2

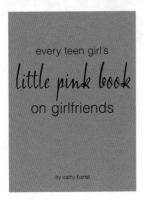

every teen girl's

little pink book

on girlfriends

by cathy bartel

find out how you can be a friend to the end...

girlfriends are great!

- wild and crazy,
- quiet and thoughtful,
- fun and exciting.

you can start being a true "girlfriend" to your gal pals:

learn the ropes

get the inside scoop

navigate clichés

stick together

learn to be real

Available at fine bookstores everywhere or at **www.harrisonhouse.com**.

Harrison House
ISBN: 1-57794-794-0